People at Work

Why are the farm workers dressed so elegantly? Why is the scholar's dog pricking up its ears? And why is the bowler-hatted man hovering in mid-air?

By looking closely at what is happening in each picture, and what the artist is trying to do, we can begin to understand and enjoy great paintings. 'People at work' is the theme of many beautiful and exciting paintings. In the pages of this book it is possible to compare eastern ideas with western, ancient with modern, and realistic with abstract. Building, harvesting, industry, office work — some activities have changed a great deal over the centuries, others hardly at all.

At the back are short biographies of the artists whose work is shown, and some practical ideas for finding out more about them.

Dr Patrick Conner is the author of several books and articles about art. He is Keeper of Fine Art at the Royal Pavilion, Art Gallery and Museums, Brighton.

Ronald Parkinson is Head of Education at the Victoria and Albert Museum, London.

LOOKING AT ART

People at Work

Patrick Conner

Consultant Editor: Ronald Parkinson
Head of Education, Victoria and Albert Museum, London

Jacket Emile Bernard, *The Buckwheat Harvest* (detail). Reproduced in full on p. 31.

Frontispiece Chaos in the classroom — a detail from Jan Steen's
A School for Boys and Girls (full picture on p.15).

© Copyright 1982 Patrick Conner

First published in 1982 by
Wayland Publishers Ltd
49 Lansdowne Place, Hove
East Sussex BN3 1HF, England

ISBN 0 85340 889 0

Phototypeset by Granada Graphics, Redhill

Printed in Italy by
G. Canale & C.S.p.A., Turin.

Contents

Looking at Art

Art is for everyone. With the help of a selection of outstanding pictures, combined with lively, down-to-earth discussion, this series shows clearly how rewarding it is to understand and enjoy paintings. Each book takes a theme, looks at the way it has been treated by famous artists from many different countries throughout the ages, and compares in simple language their varied styles and ideas.

People at Work

People at Home

Faces

List of Plates

Builders at work

A Persian castle

The active little figures in this picture are building a castle gateway in Persia — or Iran, as it is known today. They were painted by Bihzad, the greatest Persian artist of the fifteenth century; but unlike most of his fellow-artists, whose paintings showed elegant courts and enchanted gardens, Bihzad sometimes painted more down-to-earth subjects.

Here he has taken care to show the various tasks of the builders. Some cut the stone blocks to shape; others mix the mortar; others carry up the mortar in boat-shaped containers; and others set the blocks in place. Each of the twenty-one figures is hard at work.

Patterns from builders

Yet Bihzad has not tried to paint a realistic scene. He has used no effects of depth or distance; for example, the distant figures are just as large and brightly coloured as the nearer figures. His chief aim was to design an attractive pattern, based on the grid of scaffolding near the centre of the picture; and so he has used the figures as small patches of colour and movement, arranged against a golden-brown background.

Bihzad, *Building of the Castle of Khawarnaq*, c. 1494

Noah and his carpenters

This half-finished building is no ordinary house; it is Noah's Ark — and Noah himself can be seen in the centre, directing operations.

The picture was painted by an unknown Frenchman, early in the fifteenth century, for a 'Book of Hours'. In the Middle Ages, a 'Book of Hours' meant a hand-written volume which listed the prayers which should be said at each hour of the day. This particular book was first owned by John of Lancaster, Duke of Bedford, and is therefore called the *Bedford Book of Hours*.

An ark that wouldn't float?

One problem immediately occurs to us: how will this ark float? It has no hull, and it looks top-heavy. But the story of Noah's Ark told in Genesis, the first book of the Bible, does not actually say that the ark looked like a ship. According to the Bible, it was three storeys tall, and made of wood, just as this artist has shown it. And in any case, the ark would not sink, for it was built on the instructions of God — whom we can see in the sky, giving his blessing to the project.

The Flood threatens

This painting shows three different parts of the story as if they were all happening at once. First the ark is built; in the distance, the animals are rounded up; and beyond is the Flood itself, with the ships and cities which will soon be under water. Every detail is drawn with care. We can see that the carpenters' tools are similar to those used today: axes, chisels, hammers, mallets and a handsaw. One man bores holes with an auger, while another fills the holes with pegs, and Noah himself, the finest figure of all, is clearly in command of the job.

The Building of the Ark from a 15th-century *Book of Hours*.

The tower that was never finished

If Noah's Ark was the first great building project, then the second was altogether grander: the Tower of Babel. According to the Bible, Noah's sons had large families and many descendants, who all spoke the same language, until they decided to build a city and a tower, whose top would reach up to heaven. This city and tower were called Babel. But God, thinking that men and women were now becoming too proud and self-confident, made the builders start to speak in different languages, so that they no longer understood one another; they split up into different groups, and Babel was never finished.

Trouble in the top storey

Many artists have painted 'The Tower of Babel', each imagining it in his own way. This picture of a graceful white tower is another illustration from the *Bedford Book of Hours*. Once again the builders are hard at work, measuring, mixing mortar or hoisting up blocks of stone. We can recognize Noah, who is wearing the same clothes as in the ark-building scene, and who obviously disapproves of the tower. But Noah is at last approaching the end of his life (which, the Bible tells us, lasted 950 years); and the man in charge of the building, according to tradition, is his great-grandson, Nimrod, who is standing beside Noah and trying to reassure him.

At the top of the tower angels are swooping down to punish the builders, dislodging several blocks and one man. And we can see some of the men coming to blows, before going their separate ways.

The Tower of Babel from the 15th-century *Bedford Book of Hours*.

An Italian Babel

A different view of Babel can be seen in this picture in the National Gallery, London. It was painted in about 1600 by Leandro Bassano, one of a family of artists. Leandro was working in Venice, and not surprisingly his idea of the city and tower of Babel is based on the kind of buildings which he knew in Italy. This tower may be less beautiful than the one in the *Bedford Book of Hours* nearly two centuries before, but the scene is more realistic. By Leandro's time Italian artists had mastered many of the tricks of shadow and perspective which make some parts of a picture appear more distant than others; and Leandro's figures (who play a more important part than the tower) appear more rounded and solid-looking than the figures in the earlier pictures.

Refreshments on site

How different is this scene from a modern building site? Some of the tools and tasks have hardly changed since this picture was painted. But we should be surprised to see the foreman riding his horse through the thick of the building operations. And in place of a modern thermos-flask, Leandro has painted a jug of wine, with a delicate wine glass standing beside it — dangerously close to a workman's foot.

Leandro Bassano, *The Tower of Babel,* c. 1600.

In the building scenes on the last few pages, the actions of the figures, heaving, hammering or digging, have played an important part; but in these two pictures (one eastern, one western) it hardly matters how hard the men are working. In both, the artist has tried to create satisfying angles and patterns with the materials used in building.

An impossible timber yard

The picture of a carpenter's yard is a Japanese print, one of a series by Hokusai called 'The 36 Views of Mount Fuji'. This famous volcano near Tokyo is just visible in the distance, with a beam of wood pointing to its crater. No actual timber yard can ever have looked like this one: the beams standing on the right must be longer than any beams were cut at that time (about 1830), and the skyscraping pile on the left looks too neat and tall to be true. But Hokusai has formed a dramatic pattern, in which straight lines shoot up at either side and are linked by shorter, diagonal lines in between; the diagonals are the slanting roofs of the houses, the bundle of green bamboo and the propped-up block which is being sawn.

The Flying Log

Why then did Hokusai bring in any figures at all? To make the plank-patterns appear even stronger and straighter, by contrast with the figures which he has made small, hunched and comical. He has added an extra touch of wit by showing a piece of wood in mid-air on its way up to the man on top of the pile — or is it on its way down?

Katsushika Hokusai, *Carpenter's Yard*, from 'The 36 views of Mount Fuji', c. 1830.

Fleas among the girders

The Builders was painted by the modern French artist Fernand Léger. Léger was nearly seventy years old when he decided to undertake this picture. Every evening he used to travel by car past a building-site where a factory was being constructed. This, in his own words, was the idea which he wanted to paint:

> 'I saw the men swaying high up on the steel girders. I saw man as if he were a flea — he seemed lost in his own invention, with the sky above him. I wanted to show this contrast between man and his inventions, between the worker and that metal architecture, that hardness, that ironwork, those bolts and rivets.'

Although the men in his painting look strong and capable, they are dwarfed by the framework of shining steel which they have put up. Léger has coloured the girders red and yellow, to make a startling contrast with the oil-grimed workers. Moreover, the girders look extremely sharp and hard, while the figures are as bulging and shapeless as the passing clouds. We are made to feel that although the men and the clouds may come and go, the steel structure and the blue sky will last for ever.

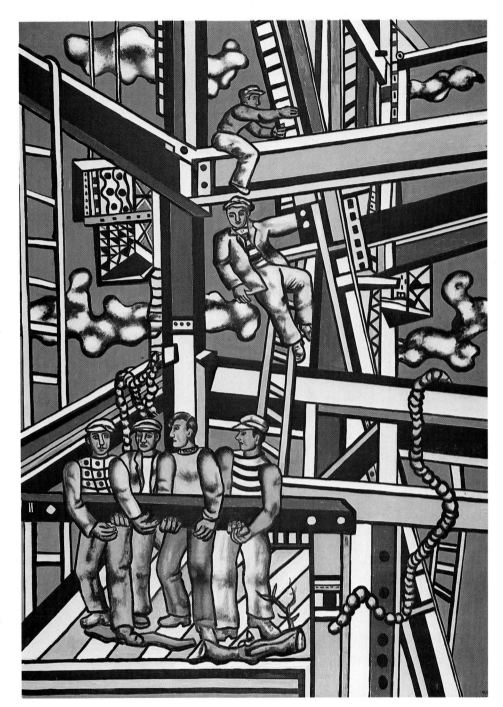

Fernand Léger, *The Builders,* 1950.

Children in school

There are many famous paintings of children at home or out of doors, but there are surprisingly few pictures which show children at work in the classroom.

Waiting for the bell

The Country School is one of these rare pictures; it is also one of the finest works by the North American artist Winslow Homer. We can almost feel what it would be like to sit in that room. The flimsy curtains over the windows are fluttering a little, suggesting a light breeze; and in spite of the curtains, a golden afternoon light is streaming into the classroom. On the right a small boy has put down his book to wipe his eyes — perhaps the schoolmistress has just spoken sharply to him. It is not the sort of sentimental picture which demands that we sympathize with the children or the teacher. But we would probably imagine that the children are a little bored, and are waiting for a bell to signal that classes are over for the day.

Confusion in class

Two hundred years before Winslow Homer painted his *Country School*, the Dutch artist Jan Steen was at work. Jan Steen was the son of a brewer, and he himself kept a tavern in later life. Most of his paintings are full of lively figures, in the street, in their houses, or (a favourite subject of Steen's) at an inn. At first glance his picture of *A School for Boys and Girls* looks rather like a drinking scene, with its swaying figures and a large

Winslow Homer, *The Country School*, 1871.

Jan Steen, *A School for Boys and Girls,* c. 1670.

jug on the floor. While the children jump on the table and do as they please, the schoolmaster sits back in his chair, cutting a quill pen, and leaving his wife to attend to the boy beside her.

Blind as an owl

On the right a boy is passing up a pair of spectacles to an owl on a perch. The point of this is that the Dutch have a proverb, 'What use are candles or spectacles if the owl does not want to see?' The proverb applies to this picture: the schoolmaster is certainly able to see what is going on, but like the owl who keeps his eyes shut all day, he chooses not to pay any attention.

Odd boy out

Jan Steen's classroom is as airy and sunny as Winslow Homer's, but it has none of Homer's atmosphere of peace. Steen has crowded his room with details, and created an effect of violent movement by making many of his figures' bodies and arms lean forwards or backwards. In the middle of the confusion is a boy who seems to belong to Homer's classroom rather than this one: he is sitting on a barrel, doggedly trying to write his exercise. But it looks as if his friends will never let him finish the page.

15

The solitary scholar

A pause for thought

Schoolchildren do most of their work in the company of others; but scholars — men and women who make studying their main occupation in life — more often work on their own. Each of these two paintings shows a scholar alone in his study.

The first picture is *The Geographer*, painted (as the signature on the wall indicates) in 1669 by the Dutch artist Johannes Vermeer. Vermeer's student of geography has spread out a map over a crumpled rug near the window, to catch the evening sunshine. There are other maps on the wall and the floor, and a globe on the cupboard. The geographer is pausing, perhaps to do some mental arithmetic. He looks thoughtful but not absent-minded; there is no danger that he will accidentally stab himself with the dividers he holds in his right hand.

Several Dutch artists painted scholars at work, but Vermeer's cool, deliberate style is particularly well suited to the subject. We feel that everything in the picture is exactly calculated, so that each brush-stroke will fall quietly but firmly in its proper place.

A miraculous moment

The scholar in this painting was a writer on religion and philosophy: Saint Augustine, Bishop of Hippo. According to tradition, Augustine was once working in his study, writing a letter to Saint Jerome to ask his opinion on a question which was worrying him — what sort of happiness could be enjoyed by souls in heaven? At that

Vittore Carpaccio, *St Augustine in his Study,* c. 1500.

moment, unknown to Augustine, Jerome was dying. Suddenly a bright light shone into Augustine's study, together with a marvellous scent, and Jerome's voice telling Augustine not to worry about matters which no human being could ever understand.

This is the episode which the Venetian artist Carpaccio has painted. Augustine is looking up at the window, amazed by the mysterious light and voice. A curly-haired dog also seems to have sensed the miracle — or is it perhaps the delicious smell?

Souvenirs of the past

The room is full of things which tell us about Augustine's life. On an altar at the far end is a mitre, to show that he was a bishop of the Church. The books on the left, and the pens (looking more like cigars) on the shelf below, make it clear that he was a scholarly writer. And

the small statues of a horse and a nude figure remind us of the active life that he enjoyed as a young man.

Musical clues

Augustine is also said to have been a composer of music; and the two sheets of music on the right give another hint of the two sides of his life. Their notes are painted so precisely that the music can actually be played. One is a piece of religious music, and the other sounds like an Italian folk-song, such as Carpaccio might have heard in Venice, sung by a passing gondolier.

(*Left*) Johannes Vermeer, *The Geographer*, 1669.

mmering iron

Furnaces in the night

Joseph Wright, who painted *An Iron Forge* in 1772, lived in England during the early years of the Industrial Revolution. He was fascinated by the many scientific discoveries that were being made at this time; and he was equally excited by the machines and factories which were using this science to produce new materials. Several of his pictures show furnaces glowing dramatically against the night sky, or (as here) lighting up the faces of an ironworker and his family. Only later, after Wright's death, did the less pleasant results of the Industrial Revolution become clear — the poverty in the industrial towns, and the long hours worked under dismal conditions in the new factories.

Spectators in the forge

In this picture, a white-hot iron bar is being held in position so that the heavy hammer will beat it into shape; the finished bar will then be sold to a blacksmith. We might find it strange that women or children should be seen in the heat, dirt and noise of a forge. But Joseph Wright thought of the shaping of the heated iron as a marvellous event, which should naturally attract spectators — even a dog.

The ironworkers appear strong and proud of their skills. But the true hero of this picture is the mechanical hammer, far more powerful than the hammer of any blacksmith. By showing the central ironworker with his arms folded, not bothering to watch the hammer fall, Joseph Wright seems to be demonstrating that machines of this kind could make life easier for working people.

Something odd in the smithy?

There are several rather awkward things about *The Blacksmith's Shop*, painted by the American Francis A. Beckett in the middle of the nineteenth century. The angles of the side window are wrongly drawn; there are fewer shadows than we should expect; and the men's heads are too large for their bodies. The artist probably had no training in art, but simply painted the events and people around him as he saw them.

This painting may not be a masterpiece, but it is nevertheless a fascinating picture. We can be sure that it shows an actual blacksmith's shop, not a scene arranged in an artist's studio. The handsome figures in *An Iron Forge* would have been drawn from hired models, but *The Blacksmith's Shop* shows the

Joseph Wright, *An Iron Forge*, 1772.

blacksmiths themselves — not particularly good-looking figures, but men with their own character and dignity.

Every detail of the smithy is included. The right-hand figure is opening and closing a huge bellows, fanning the flames which heat the iron bars. The heated bars will then be hammered on the pointed anvil, to make iron tools, horseshoes or chain: some of these are hanging on the far wall.

A dying trade

By the time of this painting, most blacksmiths were beginning to lose customers. An important part of their business was to replace the worn-out iron rims of wagon-wheels (a wheel and its rim can be seen on the right). But the railway was now taking the place of the horse-drawn wagon. This painter may have wanted to make a record of his local smithy before it changed or disappeared. Compared with the confident figures in Joseph Wright's painting, these black-smiths look a little forlorn; perhaps they, too, knew that their trade was dying.

Francis A. Beckett, *The Blacksmith's Shop,* c. 1855.

of steel

the Shaft: A Welding Heat is a picture of an iron foundry at West Point, on the Hudson River in the United States. It was painted in 1877 by an artist named John Ferguson Weir. Like Joseph Wright, Weir has conjured up an atmosphere of drama by contrasting the brilliant light of the furnace with the gloom of the forge. Dark shadows are cast over the great beams above, and a hoist like a giant bicycle chain holds up the shaft which the men are welding.

Machinery and muscle

But in this painting the heaving figures share the glory of the moment. It is a scene of heavy industry, which has no place for women or children. Even the men hold up their hands to protect their faces from the extreme heat. This building is designed for welding shafts far more massive than those hammered out in the small forge pictured by Joseph Wright. But as the picture indicates, ironworking on this huge scale still depended on human skill and muscle-power.

The glory of Newcastle

Iron and Coal was painted at about the same time as *Forging the Shaft*, but it is a more complicated picture. It is the last of eight scenes showing the history of Northumberland, in north-east England. The artist, William Bell Scott, has tried to include everything that he admired in industrial Newcastle-upon-Tyne, the chief city of the region.

Ships and locomotives

Scott has given the central position to the hammer-swinging steel-

John Ferguson Weir, *Forging the Shaft: A Welding Heat*, 1877.

William Bell Scott, *Iron and Coal*, 1861.

workers, who have the sort of muscles which other artists would have kept for pictures of Samson or Hercules. Some of the objects which they have produced lie on the ground, including a ship's anchor and a gun barrel, on which a girl sits holding her father's dinner. Behind her a pit-boy holds a Davy safety lamp and a whip for driving his pony along the coal mine. The black-coated men on the quay are shipowners. Beyond them a coal barge passes under the iron High Level Bridge constructed by the engineer Robert Stephenson, a great local hero who died just before Scott painted this picture. On the right a design for a railway engine reminds us that the locomotives for the world's first railway had been built in Newcastle by Robert's father, George Stephenson.

The picture covers four square metres, but there is hardly a space which Scott has not filled with the latest industrial products. Even the sky is occupied by a new invention — the telegraph. To make his message quite clear, Scott has added these words beneath the painting:

'In the 19th century Northumbrians show the world what can be done with iron and coal.'

21

Offices and gentlemen

Marinus, *Two Tax-Gatherers*, c. 1540.

Counting out the money

Who would want to paint a picture of men at work in an office? One possible answer is — someone who wants to mock at the officials in the painting. This is what an artist named Marinus must have had in mind when he painted this picture, usually known as *Two Tax-Gatherers*, in the sixteenth century.

The man with the account book seems to be an official of the local government, for the Dutch writing in the book sets out the amounts of tax which are to be paid by the producers of beer, fish and other foods in the district. We can only guess at what job the other man fulfils; perhaps he has collected the money from the farmers and brought it into the office.

An absurd pair

Whatever the two men are doing, it has not impressed the artist. He has made their faces wrinkled and mean-looking; the man on the right has long, curling fingers which look ready to grasp anything they can find. Most extraordinary are their feathery wigs — one red, one green. It is just possible that tax-collectors really wore this amazing headgear as a kind of official uniform; but more probably the artist was simply trying to make fun of these unpopular officials, by making them appear as ridiculous as possible.

A French artist in America

This is a more modern picture of well dressed, middle-aged men carrying out their everyday work. Once again, the artist had special reasons for painting a scene which might at first look routine and uninteresting.

The artist was Edgar Degas, a Frenchman best known as a painter of social life in Paris, the ballet, the cafés and the races. But in 1872 he crossed the Atlantic and visited New Orleans, where his mother was born and where several of his family still lived. New Orleans was the centre of the cotton industry; and the room seen in this picture is the Cotton Exchange, where businessmen bought or sold cotton in large quantities.

A hard day at the office?

It is a leisurely, relaxed scene, in which nobody seems to be hurrying. This is partly because Degas has included three of his relations in the picture. The two figures who seem to have least to do — the young man standing at the left, and the bearded man reading a newspaper — are portraits of Degas's two brothers, who did not in fact work in the Cotton Exchange. Degas's uncle, who probably did do business in the Cotton Exchange, is shown in the foreground, examining a piece of raw cotton.

By including portraits of his American relations Degas made the picture into a kind of souvenir of his visit. But it is also a painting in which the figures and the furniture have been carefully arranged. The white patches of the cotton on the table, the newspaper and the shirt-sleeve all stand out against the dark suits, while the room is coloured by the calm, warm sunlight of a Mississippi winter's day.

Edgar Degas, *The Cotton Exchange*, 1872.

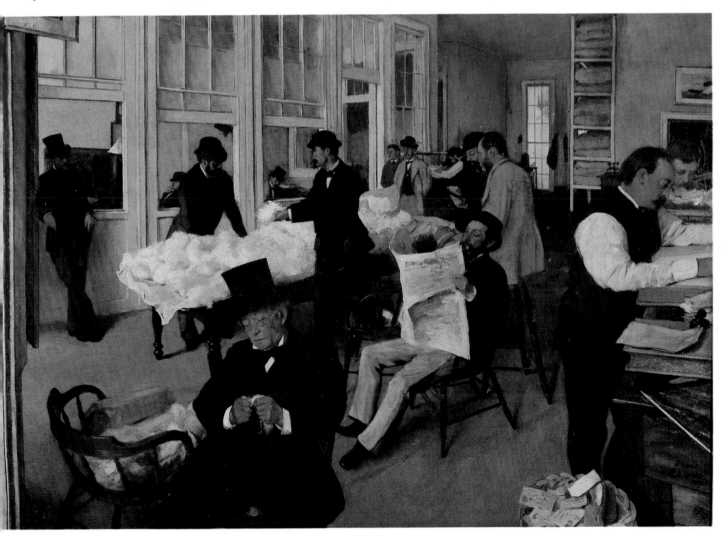

Toiling masses

Under the lash

In 1867 a young English artist named Edward Poynter created a sensation by displaying an amazing painting nearly three metres long, entitled *Israel in Egypt.* It had taken him two years to paint this picture, which illustrates the story in the Bible of how the Israelites were forced to build cities for their masters, the Egyptians. Scaffolding in the distance shows us that building is in progress; but the great feature of the painting is a grand procession, in which the Israelites are dragging a lion-headed statue to join its mate at the entrance to the city.

A long procession of people can make a dull picture. But Poynter avoided this skilfully by adding small groups to split up the main mass of figures. In one group a woman is offering a drink of water to an exhausted Israelite, and another group is pulling a hand-cart. The Egyptians are wearing fresh white clothing and hold themselves proudly upright; while the enslaved Israelites wear darker clothes or nothing at all, and their bodies are bent forward as they strain at their load.

An Egyptian epic

Poynter also chose his subject cleverly. A procession entering a city in triumph makes a stirring spectacle: scenes of this kind were repeated in the twentieth century, not as paintings but in epic films. And many people were curious to know what the great cities of ancient Egypt could have looked like; to satisfy them, Poynter studied drawings of Egyptian remains, and took care to paint the temples, the costumes and the statues as they might have appeared in Egypt three thousand years before.

Not enough manpower

It was not easy to decide how many men would have been needed to move the huge statue on its wooden rollers. In the picture as Poynter first painted it, there were fewer Israelites than we can see in the picture today. However, the painting was bought by Sir John Hawkshaw, an engineer who had himself been in Egypt to advise on the building of the Suez Canal. Hawkshaw calculated that Poynter had not provided enough hauling Israelites to move the solid stone statue. To satisfy Hawkshaw, Poynter added even more figures – those which we can see dis-appearing into the distance on the right-hand side; we can now imagine that there are hundreds more figures beyond the edge of the picture.

24

Edward Poynter, *Israel in Egypt,* 1867, the full picture above and a detail on the right.

At the factory gates

Coming from the Mill was painted in 1930 by an artist named L. S. Lowry, who lived all his life in the industrial towns of northern England. Townscapes with factories and stooping, matchstick figures are the familiar features of his pictures. In this case the factory buildings which tower above the telephone wires are more modern than those in *The Dinner Hour, Wigan* (see page 37), but they are just as forbidding, and the weather is greyer. In fact Lowry believed that his pictures were best seen after they had yellowed and darkened with age. Then the grime on the canvas would suit the soot-laden atmosphere of the subject.

Under pressure

Against the harsh background of straight lines are more than a hundred little figures, not to mention a horse, a dog and a cat. The siren at the mill has just sounded, and the mill-workers are streaming out of the factory gates, many of them in pairs or in small groups. There is no great excitement, for they are trudging home as they have trudged a thousand times before. Most of the figures are hunched forward slightly, which suggests that the weather is cold; it also makes it seem as if the weight of their massive surroundings is in some way pressing them down.

L.S. Lowry, *Coming from the Mill,* 1930.

Raining Businessmen

In this mysterious picture by the Belgian artist René Magritte, it seems to be raining bowler-hatted men. Magritte was a 'Surrealist': in other words, an artist whose clear, dream-like paintings showed objects brought together in unexpected ways, or made out of impossible materials — like a flying bird made of stone. His pictures have no single correct 'meaning'; we can look at them in whatever way we like.

In this picture the men may be moving up or down, or hovering in mid-air. They come in three standard sizes, but are otherwise alike in their city suits and coats. They are spaced at regular intervals, and pay no attention to one another. Behind every window the curtains are drawn. One idea that the painting might suggest to us is that office workers live routine lives, dressing in the same uniform and repeating the same actions every day; also, perhaps, that such men lead lonely lives without even the companionship enjoyed by the figures who work in the mill painted by Lowry.

Another puzzle

The title of this picture is another example of Magritte's particular sense of humour and love of unsolvable puzzles. He called the painting *Golconda* — which was the old name for Hyderabad, in India, a city famed for its diamonds. So 'Golconda' has come to mean 'a mine of wealth': but what does it mean here?

René Magritte, *Golconda,* 1953.

Summer in the fields

Limbourg Brothers, 'July', from *Les Très Riches Heures du Duc de Berry,* c. 1415.

Elegant harvesters

This is a picture which makes the work of a farm labourer seem the most pleasant life imaginable. It is part of a calendar painted in the fifteenth century by three French brothers named Limbourg. Beside the list of days for each month they painted a scene for that month, with precise details and clear colours which still gleam like jewels.

Like two of the paintings earlier in this book, the calendar comes from a Book of Hours — belonging this time to the Duke of Berry, who often lived in the castle shown in the picture. In front of the castle a man and a woman are removing the spring wool from the sheep's backs while across the stream two men are cutting the wheat with sickles. The wheat, speckled with red and blue flowers, falls in neat rows behind the harvester. It is a warm and peaceful scene, to which the spotless castle and the impossibly steep mountains add a fairy-tale atmosphere.

A rich blue

One colour stands out from the rest: the rich blue used for the sky and the woman's dress. The Limbourg brothers produced this blue by grinding down a precious mineral, brought from the East, called lapis lazuli. With a robe of this colour, the shearing woman appears as elegant as the courtiers who lived in the castle itself. No wonder that the Duke of Berry called this wonderfully illustrated work *Les Très Riches Heures* — 'the very rich Hours'.

Pieter Bruegel the Elder, *The Harvesters,* 1565.

Down to earth

A century and a half after the Limbourg brothers were at work, a much more down-to-earth harvesting scene was painted in the Netherlands by Pieter Bruegel. Like the Limbourgs' 'July', this was one of a series of paintings illustrating the activities of each month in the year.

This picture, called *The Harvesters,* represents August — a slightly later harvest than the French picture shows. Some men are cutting the wheat with sickles and scythes; another is tying it up into bundles; and the bundles are then carried by women to the far end of the field, where a cart takes them away. Other people are picking fruit, and we can see that some of the pears will be eaten for lunch.

Snoring in the stubble

After Pieter Bruegel had died, one of his friends described his pictures as 'hardly works of art, but works of nature'. Looking at the group around the tree, we can see what he meant. There is nothing very beautiful about the peasants eating their midday meal; if anything, Bruegel has made their faces and bodies appear broader than they really were. And the Limbourgs would never have painted a labourer flat on his back, asleep and probably snoring. Yet these figures make up a wonderfully lively scene. The misty summer landscape is imaginary; but we can easily believe in the solid little figures who are so obviously enjoying themselves.

29

George Stubbs, *Reapers*, 1784.

Controlling the reapers

The pleasant painting known as *Reapers* is set in England in the late eighteenth century; the artist was George Stubbs, a skilful painter of animals and country subjects. The same tasks are being carried out as in Bruegel's picture, and again a jug of ale stands ready. But on this occasion nobody is relaxing. An overseer, mounted on a horse, is keeping a stern eye on the harvesting. Three of the labourers are looking at him, perhaps listening to what he has to say, while the other three continue to cut or tie the corn.

A harvesting bonnet?

In several ways this picture is more artificial than Bruegel's. Stubbs's figures are clean and better dressed than farm labourers would in fact have been; the woman on the left, in particular, would never have worn such impractical headgear for a day's work in the fields. Moreover, Stubbs has placed all his figures in a line, as if they were part of a long frieze on a wall.

In short, Stubbs's figures are less realistic than Bruegel's — although they are beautifully painted, as is the horse and the landscape around them. Stubbs, and most British

artists of his time, would have thought Bruegel's peasants too ugl for a landscape like this one, whic would probably hang in the drawing-room of a wealthy family Such a family would like their pictures to show peasants who were both good-looking and well cared for; they would not want to b reminded of how poor farm labourers actually were.

Tradition in the fields

In the later years of the nineteenth century a group of French artists chose to work in Brittany, in the north-west of the country. Here the peasant farmers had to struggle to make a living from the thin soil; and several of these artists tried to capture in paint the seasonal tasks which the peasants performed as they had done for centuries. One artist in the group was Emile Bernard, whose picture *The*

Buckwheat Harvest suggests that the harvesters in their traditional costume are as natural a part of the fields as are the stacks of wheat. In this picture the figures are not individual characters, but objects which seem almost to grow out of the wheatstacks themselves.

Turning up the heat

Just as Hokusai exaggerated the length of the beams in his print of the carpenter's yard (page 12), so has Bernard exaggerated the

colours of the Brittany fields. The fierce reds and yellows give an impression of intense heat – the sun seems to have burnt all green out of the wheat. And the crude, dark outlines drawn around the figures and stacks match the primitive, rhythmical action of the harvesting.

Emile Bernard, *The Buckwheat Harvest,* 1888.

Partnerships

The most famous carpenter

Christ in the Carpenter's Shop is the work of a remarkable artist, Georges de La Tour. After his death La Tour's paintings were forgotten for more than two centuries. Only recently have his magical candlelit scenes been recognized and admired.

In this picture, Joseph the carpenter is turning the handle of an auger to bore a hole in a block of wood. A mallet, a chisel and a shaving of wood lie on the floor. Jesus, shown as a boy of about ten years old, is holding a candle in his fingertips, so that the melting wax will not run down his hand; with his other hand he is shielding the flame. Most of the candlelight seems to fall on the face of Jesus.

A still moment

Although Joseph is bent over his auger, this is not a scene of strenuous activity. The straight candle-flame indicates that he is breathing gently, for even a moderate breath of air would surely make the flame flicker. It is a quiet moment, shut off from the outside world. Neither figure is watching the task in progress; each is lost in his own thoughts. Perhaps Jesus is thinking how different his work will be from Joseph's. But La Tour has added one little detail which suggests that Jesus has actually been helping Joseph at his workbench: there are dirty fingernails on the boy's red-glowing left hand.

Holes for potatoes

In La Tour's painting the two figures stand close to each other, making us aware of the close relationship between Joseph and Jesus. But in Jean-François Millet's picture *Planting Potatoes*, the two figures are a little farther apart — and we no longer have the feeling that there is any special relationship or affection between them.

Peasants at work in the fields, generally wearing the heavy clogs shown here, provided the subjects of many of Millet's paintings. The man in this picture is a little better dressed than the ragged labourers whom Millet often painted. This man may well be farming a plot of land which he owns himself. As he pulls up each clod of earth with his hoe, his wife plants a handful of potatoes. Their faces are in shadow, showing no particular emotion. They are simply two people doing an ordinary job.

Georges de La Tour, *Christ in the Carpenter's Shop. c.* 1640.

Tied to the soil

Millet was a Frenchman, working in the middle years of the nineteenth century, at a time of bitter political struggle. Some people admired Millet's paintings of bowed-down, humble peasants, because they thought that these pictures amounted to an attack on the French government for making the peasants' life so wretched. Millet was content for his pictures to be considered in this way. But he was a peasant's son who felt that the changing seasons and the growing crops enslaved the peasants as brutally as any government could. Just as night follows day, Millet seems to say, so must the woman plant potatoes as her husband lifts the soil; there is no escape.

Jean-François Millet, *Planting Potatoes,* c. 1861.

Women at work

A jealous calf

This picture of a woman milking a cow was painted in the early part of the thirteenth century − which means that it is the oldest picture in this book. With one hand the woman is holding a wooden bucket by its handle; with the other she is milking the cow. The cow, which is tethered to a post by a rope, is licking her calf.

It is a simple and charming scene, painted by an artist whose name is not known. The picture comes from a bestiary − that is, a hand-written book (often illustrated) describing the features of various animals, and drawing from each one a moral for human behaviour. The painter of this picture was not a great artist; he has made the cow's milk, for example, twist and bend in a very strange way, and both the woman and the calf seem to be stepping over the painted border at the edge of the picture. But the artist must have had a considerable sense of humour. Although the calf is being licked by its mother, it is objecting strongly to something; perhaps it feels that its mother should be giving her milk to her calf, and not to the serious-looking milkmaid.

Alone in the kitchen

A much more realistic trickle of milk can be seen in *A Maidservant Pouring Milk*, which was painted by Johannes Vermeer a few years before he produced *The Geographer* (see page 16). Like the geographer, this maid is entirely absorbed in her work, unaware that anyone can see her. As we look at the picture we seem almost like spies.

Vermeer has not tried to make either the maid or the room especially pretty. The bare wall is decorated only with a narrow strip of patterned Dutch tiles in place of skirting board. We can see nails and old nail holes, and patches of damp under the window. The small box on the floor was a useful gadget in a cold kitchen: it was used as a foot-warmer. Hot coals would be placed in a dish inside it and the maid could then put the box under her feet, which would be warmed through the holes in the box top.

As solid as a loaf

We can certainly imagine how the objects in the picture would feel to the touch − the rim of the earthenware jug, for example, or the surface of the wholemeal bread, which Vermeer has sprinkled with little dots of white paint, giving a slightly sugary texture to the crust. Everything in the picture looks solid, most of all the girl herself. Whereas the woman milking her cow had a flat, cardboard appearance, Vermeer's maid is as well rounded as the loaf of bread in her basket.

Woman milking a Cow, from a 13th-century bestiary.

Johannes Vermeer, *A Maidservant pouring Milk,* c. 1660.

Washing the pots

This girl is doing an even less glamorous job: washing up. The picture, painted in 1738, is known as *The Scullery Maid* ('scullery' meaning a room in which kitchen pots were kept). The maid is standing over an upturned wooden vat, cleaning a long-handled frying pan with a handful of straw.

The artist was Jean-Baptiste Chardin, a Frenchman who had become famous for his paintings of still-life — that is, arrangements of everyday objects such as plates, bottles and fruit. All the kitchen utensils in this picture (vase, copper pot, ladle, vat, frying pan and earthenware casserole) had already appeared in still-life pictures by Chardin. But now Chardin has added the figure of a maid. The result is not very different from a still-life. The girl seems neither happy nor angry with her work; she is leaning forward, but there is no feeling of movement. Chardin seems to regard her as another interesting kitchen object, included in order to make up a satisfying combination of shapes.

Colour in the scullery

The Scullery Maid is certainly a pleasure to look at. Chardin has managed to suggest the difference between the soft cotton of the girl's skirt and blouse, and the stiffer linen of her apron. Her clothes are painted in a beautiful range of creamy colours, set against the darker browns around her, while a few small patches of brighter colour catch the eye: the green of the casserole, the maid's blue ribbon and petticoat, and a touch of red on her lips.

Jean-Baptiste Chardin, *The Scullery Maid*, 1738.

Women at the mill

What is unusual about this picture, painted in 1874 by an artist named Eyre Crowe? Before this time, artists had shown women working on the farm, or in shops, or at home; but they had never shown women who worked in a factory — although women had been employed in factories for many years, usually because they could be paid less than men.

Not fit to be painted?

Crowe's picture is called *The Dinner Hour, Wigan*. When it was first displayed at the Royal Academy in London, many visitors thought it ugly and offensive. They did not want to be reminded of what the industrial towns of northern Britain were like. We would probably agree that the smoking cotton-mills of Wigan do not make a beautiful scene; but even in these bleak surroundings, Crowe has made the life of a factory girl appear more pleasant than it really was. The women all look young, healthy and pretty, and Crowe has shown them enjoying their lunch-break on a sunny day. If he had wanted to paint a more typical view of their working life, he might well have shown them hard at work inside the factory, with oilstains on their aprons and rain pouring down outside.

The painting leaves us with some unanswered questions. A policeman stands at the street junction: what kind of trouble is he expecting? And when the dinner hour is over, what will happen to the baby by the lamp-post?

Eyre Crowe, *The Dinner Hour, Wigan*, 1874.

Russian First World War poster, 1916.

A poster with a message

This Russian poster shows a young woman at work in a factory. The name of the artist who designed the poster is not known, but we can be certain that he or she wanted those who saw it to admire the woman and what she was doing.

The poster was printed in 1916, during the First World War, at a time when millions of Russian soldiers had already been killed. Men who would normally have been working in factories were serving in the army or navy instead, so that women were urgently needed to take their places in the factories. The machinery shown here was probably used for producing armaments; and the poster appealed to those Russians who still had money to lend to the Russian government. The Russian words read:

Everything for the war!
Subscribe to the 5½% war loan.

As we have seen on the last page, some of those who saw *The Dinner Hour, Wigan* were shocked by the sight of women who worked in a factory. But this poster was designed to do just the opposite — to make people feel proud to be taking part in the same war effort as the girl in the picture. The message which the poster suggests is that if you lend your money to the government, it will be well spent — on modern machinery, carefully operated by attractive women doing their heroic duty for Russia.

A war artist in the factory

In the Second World War, women were again in demand for jobs which they would not have undertaken in peace time. This picture, entitled *Aero-engine Accessories Girls,* was painted by the English artist Dorothy Coke. She was one of several painters who were appointed official War Artists in 1940; their task was to paint or draw pictures which recorded the war in all its aspects — including battles, bomb sites, and soldiers off duty. As a War Artist, Dorothy Coke chose to paint these women working in a factory, making parts for aeroplane engines to be used by the Royal Air Force.

Girls without faces

Unlike the Russian poster, this picture is not trying to make anyone support the war. The girls here are less glamorous than the Russian girl; their boiler-suits are shapeless, and we cannot even see their faces, which are covered by gasmasks to prevent their breathing in poisonous fumes. On the other hand the artist is not protesting about women working in a factory. She has painted this picture simply as an interesting and unusual scene, making full use of the circle and cylinder shapes, the angled lamps, and the different postures of the five women at work.

Dorothy Coke, *Aero-engine Accessories Girls,* 1941.

The most unpleasant job

John Brett, *The Stonebreaker*, 1857.

Of all the manual jobs which a man could undertake in the nineteenth century, breaking up stones was thought to be the worst. Stone-breaking meant hard, monotonous, unskilled labour, fit for convicts or the very poor who could find no other way to earn a few pence.

These two English pictures of stonebreakers were painted in exactly the same year: 1857. Once again they show how very differently two artists could treat the same subject.

The boy stone-breaker

The saddest thing about the first picture is that the stonebreaker is so young. It can hardly be this boy's own fault that he has nothing more satisfying to do. The words 'London 23 miles', written on a milestone at the left of the picture, remind us that there is work not far away — for other people, but not for the boy.

On the other hand it is difficult to feel very sorry for the young stone-breaker in this picture. We soon stop looking at him and start to

40

(*Right*) Henry Wallis, *The Stonebreaker*, 1857.

admire the bright detail of the dog, the plants, the hills and the pieces of flint beside the boy. The artist, John Brett, was in fact fascinated by geology, and he has clearly used his knowledge of the forms of rocks and stones in this picture. But the all-over sharpness of detail, and the pleasantness of the landscape, tend to distract our attention from the boy himself.

Down and out

The second painting, by Henry Wallis, also offers a spectacular landscape, but in this case the main interest of the picture lies in the stonebreaker himself. He has actually died of exhaustion while at work. The hammer has slipped from his grasp, but there is nobody to see what has happened. The calm twilight seems to make the event even more tragic.

Neither of the stonebreakers, however, is quite alone. The younger figure has a small terrier to keep him company, although it seems more occupied with chewing the lining of its master's cap. The old stonebreaker's companion is more unexpected: a weasel, which would never have dared to come near the man while he was alive, has now crept up to his outstretched boot.

Who was responsible?

When Wallis's picture was put on exhibition in London, he added a quotation beneath the picture, which included the words, 'For us was thy back so bent, for us were thy straight limbs and fingers so deformed. . . .' Wallis was criticizing the harsh laws and unsympathetic attitudes towards the poor which, he felt, were the real cause of the miserable life and death of the stonebreaker.

Men and machines

The pictures on these pages have similar titles: *The Knife-Grinder* and *The Scissors-Grinder*. The picture on the left was painted in 1887; the one on the right was painted only twenty-five years later, in 1912. Yet the pictures could hardly be more different in style. Comparing them, we can see how ideas about art changed dramatically in the very early years of the twentieth century.

Hard times

The old man on the left looks as if he has spent his whole life wheeling his knife-sharpening machine along village streets. Travelling knife-grinders could not expect to earn much money, especially at a time when new, mass-produced knives were becoming cheap to buy. In this picture two very well dressed children watch the shabby, elderly figure as he holds a knife against the grinding-wheel, which he is spinning by working a foot-pedal. The artist, a British painter named James Charles, seems to have regarded his knife-grinder as a picturesque relic of old-fashioned country life.

The vibrating man

When you first set eyes on the picture on the right, it seems to be nothing but a confused jumble. Then, as you look more closely, the figure of a scissors-grinder can be made out crouching over his wheel. But the artist – the Russian Kasimir Malevich – had no interest in simply painting objects in a recognizable way. He has shown the man's arms, legs and scissors three or four times, making him look as if the machine is shaking him violently, or as if several frames of a film are being shown at the same time.

Metal kneecaps

There is nothing shabby about this character. The background of tube-shapes and beam-shapes indicates that he works in a factory. Everything seems to be made of polished metal, even his pointed elbows and kneecaps. By splitting up the picture into small sharp pieces, Malevich suggests that the man, the grinding-wheel and the factory are all part of the same huge machine.

(*Left*) James Charles, *The Knife-grinder*, 1887.

(*Right*) Kasimir Malevich, *The Scissors-grinder*, 1912.

New art for a new age

How then did Malevich think of his scissors-grinder? He painted this picture at a time when many Russians believed that factory workers, in control of their machinery, were about to create a new and fair government in which working people became their own masters. So his knife-grinder represents not a bygone age but hope for a glorious future.

In each of these two pictures the artist's style suits his attitude to the subject. The first is painted in a straightforward, traditional manner, with loving attention paid to the old house and garden. Malevich, on the other hand, has ignored all such details in his effort to transmit one powerful idea — the idea of the shuddering, gleaming machine.

The artists in this book

Note: 'c.', short for the Latin word *circa*, means 'about'; so 'c.1440-c.1515' means that the artist was born in about 1440, and died in about 1515.

BASSANO, LEANDRO (1557-1622), also called Leandro dal Ponte. He and his family were brought up in Bassano in Italy (from which they received their name), but then moved to Venice where he painted *The Tower of Babel* (page 11).

BECKETT, FRANCIS A., a little-known American artist active in the mid-nineteenth century, was born in the West Indies and was, during the 1860s, an inmate of the State Insane Asylum at Stockton in the United States. His *The Blacksmith's Shop* (on page 19) is the only picture of his to have come to light.

BERNARD, EMILE (1868-1941) was a French artist whose style continued to change as his work progressed. In the years 1888-91 he and his friend Gauguin painted several brilliantly coloured pictures of Brittany, including *The Buckwheat Harvest* (*Le Blé Noir*) shown on page 31.

BIHZAD (*c.* 1440-*c.*1515) was a Persian who painted portraits and finely detailed illustrations for manuscript books. *The Building of the Castle at Khawarnaq* (page 8) is taken from one such manuscript (the *Khamsa*, or five poems, by Nizami).

BRETT, JOHN (1831-1902) was an English painter of landscapes and seascapes. In *The Stonebreaker* (page 40), his best-known work, John Brett used his younger brother as a model for the boy.

BRUEGEL, PIETER (*c.*1530-1569) is usually called 'Pieter Bruegel the elder', because one of his sons ('Pieter Bruegel the younger') had the same name. He created many vivid pictures of Flemish life, such as *The Harvesters* (page 29), as well as bloodthirsty scenes of warfare and monsters.

CARPACCIO, VITTORE (*c.*1455-*c.*1525) combined strong colours (which were typical of many other Venetian artists) with clear details and a sense of humour. *St Augustine in his Study* (page 17) is one of a series of his paintings in the Scuola di San Giorgio degli Schiavoni, Venice.

CHARDIN, JEAN-BAPTISTE (1699-1779), who painted *The Scullery Maid* (page 36), lived in Paris for almost all his life. His pictures show everyday objects, and ordinary people carrying out their daily tasks.

CHARLES, JAMES (1851-1906) was a British artist who painted portraits, landscapes and scenes of everyday life, such as *The Knife-Grinder* (page 42).

COKE, DOROTHY (1897-1980) was an English artist best known for her watercolours. She painted *Aero-engine Accessories Girls* (page 39), as an official War Artist.

CROWE, EYRE (1824-1910) won a reputation for painting the less glamorous side of life in Victorian England (see *The Dinner Hour, Wigan*, page 37) and also in the United States.

DEGAS, EDGAR (1834-1917) painted life in nineteenth-century Paris, and especially its women — working, washing, or dancing. His *Portraits in an Office: the Cotton Exchange* (page 23) dates from a visit to the United States in 1872.

HOKUSAI, KATSUSHIKA (1760-1849) was one of the greatest printmakers in Japan — a country where the art of printing, especially from wood-blocks, was developed more highly than in any other country. 'The 36 Views of Mount Fuji' (one of which, *The Carpenter's Yard*, is shown on page 12) was his masterpiece; and several western artists imitated his way of arranging shapes and colours.

HOMER, WINSLOW (1836-1910) was a highly successful painter of the life and landscape of North America. He painted *The Country School* (page 14) in 1871, in a small town in New York State.

LA TOUR, GEORGES DE (1593-1652) worked for most of his life in Lorraine, which was a part of Germany until France took it over in 1630. *Christ in the Carpenter's Shop* (page 32) is one of his magically distinctive paintings.

LÉGER, FERNAND (1881-1955) was one of the leading French artists of the twentieth century. Many of his paintings show figures or places split up into small, sharp, solid shapes. *The Builders* — or *Les Constructeurs* — (page 13) is in a museum devoted to his work, the Musée National Fernand Léger, Biot, France.

LIMBOURG: the three brothers, Pol (or Paul), Jean (or John) and Herman de Limbourg worked for the Dukes of Burgundy in France, including the Duke of Berry, in the early fifteenth century. *Les Très Riches Heures du Duc de Berry* is a 'Book of Hours' which contains a picture for each month for the year; *July* is on page 28.

LOWRY, L. S. (1887-1976), best known for his crowded industrial landscapes, was brought up in Manchester; but *Coming from the Mill* (page 26) is in the Art Gallery of Salford, the town where he lived for most of his life.

MAGRITTE, RENÉ (1898-1967) was a Belgian artist, whose 'impossible' objects and combinations made him one of the best known Surrealist painters. *Golconda* is on page 27.

MALEVICH, KASIMIR (1878-1935) was a Russian artist active in the years 1910-20, a time of political and artistic revolution in Russia. *The Scissors-Grinder* (page 43) was painted in 1912; in 1913 Malevich began to paint completely abstract arrangements of lines, triangles and rectangles.

MARINUS VAN REYMERSWAELE (c.1500-c.1570) worked in the Netherlands. He painted a number of grotesque figures, such as *Two Tax-Gatherers* (page 22).

MILLET, JEAN-FRANCOIS (1814-1875) was the son of peasant farmers, and became the greatest painter of peasants at work. *Planting Potatoes* is on page 33.

POYNTER, SIR EDWARD (1836-1919) was born in Paris but spent most of his life in Britain. Many of his paintings were imaginary scenes of life in the ancient world. A famous example is *Israel in Egypt* (page 24-5).

SCOTT, WILLIAM BELL (1811-1890) was master of Newcastle's School of Design, which trained young men to design attractive objects which could be mass-produced in factories. An advertisement for this school can be found in the newspaper in the lower right corner of his *Iron and Coal* (page 21). The paintings of Northumbrian history, including *Iron and Coal* (1861), surround the inner courtyard of Wallington Hall, Cambo, Northumberland — a National Trust property which is generally open to the public.

STEEN, JAN (1626-1679), who painted *A School for Boys and Girls* (page 15), gained such a reputation for his lively, homely scenes that in Holland an untidy house full of active people is still called 'a Jan Steen household'.

STUBBS, GEORGE (1724-1806) — see *Reapers* on page 30 — was an English painter of portraits and animal pictures, especially horses.

VERMEER, JOHANNES (1632-1675), a great Dutch artist, specialized in views of towns and in calm figures seen in small rooms or courtyards, such as *The Geographer* (page 16) and *A Maidservant Pouring Milk* (page 35).

WALLIS, HENRY (1830-1916), an English artist, is chiefly known for two paintings: *The Stonebreaker* (page 41), and *The Death of Chatterton* (shown in another book in this series, *People at Home*).

WEIR, JOHN FERGUSON (1841-1928) of the United States — painter of *Forging the Shaft: A Welding Heat* (page 20) — was the son of a better-known American artist, Robert Walker Weir.

WRIGHT, JOSEPH (1734-1797), often known as 'Joseph Wright of Derby', was an English painter of portraits, landscapes, industrial scenes and scientific experiments. *An Iron Forge* (page 18) is in the Mountbatten collection at Broadlands House, Hampshire, a house which is open to the public for much of the summer.

Finding out more

Books

Most public libraries and some school libraries have a section of art books with good colour reproductions on particular artists, periods or styles. Take out those which include artists from this book or others whose work you admire. Apply a critical eye.

Art galleries

It is better, of course, to see the real thing. Go round an art gallery and study a *few* pictures – those which catch your attention or which have been painted by an artist you have read about. Art galleries and museums will give information about the pictures in their collection. Some have an Education Officer, and many arrange films and talks on art and artists.

Acknowledgements

The author and publishers gratefully acknowledge those who have lent pictures which appear on the following pages:

The British Library 8, The British Museum 9, 10, 12; courtesy of the Trustees, The National Gallery, London 11, 22; Musée National Fernand Léger, Biot, France – photo Jacques Mer 13 © SPADEM, Paris 1981; The St Louis Art Museum (Missouri, USA) 7; Duke of Sutherland Collection, on loan to the National Gallery of Scotland – photo Tom Scott 15 and *frontispiece*; Städelsches Kunstinstitut, Frankfurt am Main – Kunst-Dias Blauel 16; Scuola di S. Giorgio degli Schiavoni – photo Alinari 10; Mountbatten Collection, Broadlands House, Hants. 18; National Gallery of Art, Washington D.C., gift of Edgar William and Bernice Chrysler Garbisch 19; © 1965 Metropolitan Museum of Art, gift of Lyman G. Bloomingdale, 1901 20; © 1981 Metropolitan Museum of Art, Rogers Fund 1919 – photo Eric Pollitzer 29; Wallington Hall, Cambo, National Trust – photo Turner's 21; Musée des Beaux-Arts – photo Marie-Louise Perony 23; Guildhall, London – photo Cooper-Bridgeman Library 24; City of Salford Art Gallery and Museum – photo Derek Seddon 26; Menil Foundation, Inc. 27 © AD'AGP, Paris 1981; Musée Conde, Chantilly – photo Giraudon, Paris 28; The Tate Gallery London 30; Josefowitz Collection, Switzerland 31 and jacket; Cliche Musées Nationaux, Paris 32; courtesy Museum of Fine Arts, Boston, gift of Quincy Adams Shaw, 17. 1505 33; Bodleian Library, Ms. Bodley 764, folio 41 34; Rijksmuseum, Amsterdam 35; Hunterian Art Gallery, University of Glasgow 36; City of Manchester Art Galleries 37, 42; Imperial War Museum 38; Brighton Pavilion, Art Gallery and Museums 39; The Walker Art Gallery, Liverpool 40; courtesy of Birmingham Museums and Art Gallery 41; Yale University Art Gallery, gift of Collection Société Anonyme 43.

Index